MISS BEST'S
Etiquette for Young People

Miss Alyse Best

PEP
PresS

Portland Entertainment Publishing, Inc.

Printed in the United States of America
First PEP PresS Printing: November 1990
10987654321

PEP PresS
Portland Entertainment Publishing, Inc.
114 SW Second Avenue
Portland, Oregon 97204

ISBN 0-945033-02-8
Library of Congress Catalog Card # 90-63184

Cover photo by Franklin Hill
Cover design by Carlene Lynch and Franklin Hill

Editing, layout, and design by Kathy Jo Noack, Kathy VanderHouwen,
and Colleen Kelley; VanderHouwen & Associates, Inc., Macintosh Business
Services; Portland, Oregon.

Attention: Schools and Corporations

PEP PresS books are available at quantity discounts with bulk purchase
for educational, business, or sales promotional use.

For information, please write to
PEP PresS at the above address.

Miss Best's Views On Etiquette

Most parents of today were raised during times when the word "etiquette" was as foreign as the word "proper." As they have reached maturity, they have come to realize the important relationship between good manners and business savvy. These same parents have paid hundreds of dollars for their children to attend Miss Best's etiquette seminars because they feel that in order for their children to be as successful in life as they want to be, they must learn proper etiquette at a young age.

Miss Best's Etiquette for Young People was written for this very reason. It is written from the viewpoint of young people aged 6 to 16, teaching them how to behave in the social settings they will face as well as how to act toward others in a kinder, more polite manner without losing their peers' respect. The foremost purpose of this book is to build a feeling of self-confidence, maturity, and a desire to be the most successful person you choose to be.

As Miss Best continues expanding into Protocol consulting and instructing adults in corporate, social, and wedding etiquette, she has come to realize more than ever the importance of teaching etiquette to children in their formative years in a fun, relaxing way.

Miss Best is the Founder and Chief Executive Officer of Best Protocol, which has offices in Arcadia, California; Pittsburgh, Pennsylvania; Washington, D.C.; and Palm Beach, Florida. In 1984, she worked as Protocol Officer for the Summer Olympics, hosting many foreign dignitaries such as H.R.H. Prince Philip of Great Britain and H.R.H. Princess Nora of Liechtenstein, and just recently completed an appointment as White House Liaison for the Foster Grandparent Program in Washington, D.C.

Miss Best hopes that people of all ages will find the following pages useful in their everyday lives as well as when they are in social settings.

Respectfully yours,

Miss Alyse Best

Note to parents on how to use Miss Best's book with their children:

Ages 6 to 10: Read through the book with your children. Do the role-playing with them and encourage their use of proper etiquette by complimenting them when they do things properly. Make the games fun!!

Ages 11 to 13: Try to answer questions they may have about use of proper etiquette in certain situations. Encourage them to use the suggestions in the book with their friends without feeling uncomfortable. Help them with the role-playing exercises. Remind them to use this book as a reference as situations start coming up when their social life starts to expand in their teens.

Ages 14 to 16: Read this book before you give it to them! You might be surprised at how many basic rules of etiquette we parents seem to forget over the years, especially since we were not lucky enough to have this book at our children's ages. Then leave them alone with this book unless they ask for you to participate with them. Simply give compliments often when you see them using this new information. If they appear nervous about attending a social event, you could offer a gentle reminder that any questions they might have will be listed in Miss Best's book. Better yet, encourage them to write to Miss Best and ask for her advice.

*I lovingly dedicate this book to my children,
Lanah and Tristan, who have been the inspiration for
every page. Being the child of an etiquette instructor
is truly as difficult as being the preacher's kid, but
they have remained wonderful through it all.*

Miss Alyse Best

Contents

OVERVIEW

Etiquette
for Young People

When you think of "etiquette," you might think only of dry rules about which fork to use when you're having dinner with your Great-Aunt Lydia. But etiquette means more than that. It is the manners you already use every day, with your family at home, with your friends at parties or in school, or at the church or synagogue, as well as at dinner in a restaurant (with or without Great-Aunt Lydia). Maybe you don't think much about your manners. But every person you meet, your family and your friends, will treat you according to the way you treat them — your manners — your *etiquette*.

Proper etiquette can help to make others feel comfortable around us. Don't you like being around people who treat other people (like you!) well? A knowledge of proper manners can also make *us* feel comfortable and secure around others.

Through the chapters of this book, you will learn the importance of the unspoken proper manners. Learning them can be helpful to you for the rest of your life, and it can be fun, too! As you read the book, sometimes you will realize that you are already using proper etiquette. Other things

1

might be very new to you. Don't worry if you have to read some parts more than once to get them down and start using them.

Someday, maybe some of you will travel to foreign countries and notice how differently people act from Americans. Or maybe some of you already have travelled outside the United States. Did you notice that people there were comfortable with things that you were not? Here are just a few major etiquette differences:

1. In **Fiji**, it is offensive to look someone directly in the eye when you are not talking to them.

2. If someone in **Zimbabwe** gives you a gift, you *must* receive it with both hands.

3. Crossing your legs when sitting is very offensive in **Thailand.** It is also offensive to place one's arm over the back of someone else's chair.

4. In **Taiwan**, winking is improper. In **Nigeria**, it means you wish someone to leave the room.

5. A man is not a gentleman if he holds his hands in his pockets while speaking in **Switzerland**.

6. In **Nigeria**, you must not receive even one piece of paper in your left hand because of the bad meanings it suggests.

I wonder which of our manners people from other countries would find unusual. Think about it. I'm sure that there are some.

Americans love to read about Princess Diana and Prince Charles. They seem to lead very special, enchanted lives. We can only dream about living their lives because in Great Britain one has to be *born* royal to *be* royal.

In this country our "royalty" includes presidents, first ladies, governors, senators, members of congress, and other elected or important officials. No matter how you were born, there's a possibility that *you* can grow up to become the most important person in the United States — the President — or anyone you choose to be.

I t's important to remember that no matter what you choose to be someday, good manners will always help. It will help when meeting teachers, friends, parents, and even future in-laws. It will help you feel more confident when you date, attend a party, or host your own party.

You can grow up to be the person you want to become in a large part because of your manners. That's right! Everyone is going to act towards you in a certain way because of your manners. If you believe in yourself, let others know you do by how you walk and talk. Treat others with respect and courtesy. Study hard. If you do all of these things, you have your ticket to be whatever you want to be, and be happier and more confident in whatever you do.

Remember that most people are shy, especially young people. If you *act* as if you are not, no one will know unless you tell them. Speaking with a pleasant, strong, clear voice lets others know that you are someone they should pay attention to. You want to be loud enough for others to hear you, but not so loud that you are annoying. One way to know if your volume is at a good level is to notice how adults react to you. Do they constantly tell you to lower or to raise your voice? If you hear either one of those comments, you know that you need to adjust the volume of your voice. Part of good manners is knowing that there are different levels of speech for different situations. An example might be the level you use in the cafeteria with your friends compared to the level at the dinner table with your grandparents.

Much of proper etiquette is acting. Good manners come from the goodness within us, because we truly respect and want to be kind to others. There are times, however, when we are not feeling our best or when we really do not want to do something. We must simply act out good manners at times such as these. An

3

example of this would be when you have to meet and shake hands with that strange boy with the long, stringy hair. Another would be when your neighbor fixes chicken livers especially for your visit, so you have to eat them, or when you receive a box of stationery from your Aunt Connie instead of the gold necklace you thought she had been hinting at.

The more you practice good manners during difficult situations, the more natural it will become. In each chapter is a sticky situation, called Let's Pretend, in which you'll meet the Herkelschmertz family — Tristan, Lanah, Beau, and Morgan, (and of course Mr. and Mrs. Herkelschmertz). You will get to practice choosing then what our friends the Herkelschmertzes should do in those times when they find themselves suddenly "on the spot." Each chapter also has Role-Playing Exercises with ideas for other ways to practice good etiquette. A quiz at the end will help you see how much you've learned.

As you put good manners into practice in your life, soon you will start to enjoy being kind towards others. Remember first of all that kindness is the reason behind all etiquette. This will help you to remember the most important etiquette rule of all: NEVER correct anyone else's manners.

"So Nice to Meet You"

An introduction is very important. It may be the only time you touch another person's life. You are sharing who you are, and during this brief moment that person will unconsciously make judgments about what you are like. Practice these few simple rules about introductions, and every person you meet will remember something good about you.

1. When you meet people, look directly into their eyes. Are you going to remember people who shyly look down at their feet and mumble "hello"? Or will you remember better someone who looks you directly in the eye? Of course, you will remember the person with whom you had eye contact! People now know they need to pay attention to you. Haven't you met people you thought were snobby at first, only to find that they were simply shy? Nice people might not be able to show that they are friendly if they first come across as being snobby.

2. Smile. How simple, but how important! Smile, and people will judge you as being friendly — the same way you would judge others.

3. Hold your hand out and shake theirs. Handshakes are symbols of warmth and acceptance. Not too long ago, it was improper for a gentleman to hold out his hand for a lady's handshake. She had to do it first. Now, either one can do it and both should immediately.

We often judge people's personalities by the way they shake hands, although this is not always fair. A gentleman is thought to be wimpy if he has a limp handshake, and a woman is thought to be cold and dull if she has the same. Stretch out your hand and receive the other's with the whole hand, interlocking the thumbs and gripping warmly — not loosely and not too tightly. Shake gently up and down several times and then let go.

4. Say something like, "How do you do?" or "Nice to meet you," and end by repeating their names. "How do you do, Ms. Murphy?" When you do this, it's a compliment to the people you are meeting. Not because *they* like to hear their names, but because it will help *you* to remember them, and that is one of the greatest compliments.

Concentrate on each name when you do and relate it to the person in some way. You might be able to remember Stewart's name by imagining a piece of stew on his shirt. You could remember Mrs. Shepherd's name by seeing her in your mind with some sheep and a staff. (But make sure you don't get mixed up and call her Mrs. Bo-peep!)

All young people should call adults by their last names unless asked to do differently. If you are addressing a woman and you are not sure whether she's married or not, use "Ms." instead of "Mrs." or "Miss."

Here are some more rules for introductions that you need to memorize.

1. If a person has a title, such as a doctor, a reverend, or someone with military rank, never use Mr., Mrs., or Ms. Always use the title.

Yes	No
Dr. Carter	Mr. Carter
Lt. Maio	Ms. Maio
Rev. Jackson	Mr. Jackson

If a person is a political figure such as a city commissioner, mayor, governor, senator, or president, only use Mr., Mrs., or Ms. in connection with the title. Otherwise, use the title with the name.

Yes	Yes	No
Commissioner Bogle	Mr. Commissioner	Mr. Bogle
Governor Johnson	Mr. Governor	Mr. Johnson
Senator Crocker	Madam Senator	Mrs. Crocker
President Bush	Mr. President	Mr. Bush

2. When introducing a man and a woman (or a boy and a girl), the woman's name comes first. (Ladies first.) When introducing your friends to each other who are both girls or both boys, either name can come first, as long as there is not a major age difference.

3. The older person's name comes first when introducing a younger person to an older person. (Age before beauty — oops!)

4. When introducing an important person to either a man or a woman, the important person's name comes first. (Mr. President, may I present Miss Lanah Hamilton. Lanah, I would like you to meet the President.)

At some time you will probably meet a handicapped person, such as a person in a wheelchair. Of course you already know better than to make fun of handicapped people or point at them and whisper with your friends about them. Do not stare at them either. Try to make them feel included in whatever is going on. Many public places now have improvements like special ramps to adapt to the handicapped. Be patient with them if it takes them longer than you to do something. Don't jump in and do things for them unless they ask for your help. It may be important to them to do things for themselves whenever they can, so don't take that away from them. Remember that they probably know very well what they are doing, and you may only get in their way!

"Let's Pretend . . ."

Lanah Herkelschmertz looks happily around at the party going on in the Herkelschmertz living room. Her guests are munching on chips and pretzels and sodas near the table of refreshments and talking in comfortable little groups. When the doorbell rings, Lanah brings her newest guest, Linda from summer camp, through the hall to three of her school friends standing in the doorway to the living room.

"Linda," says Lanah, "I'd like you to meet my friends, Stacy, Erika, and…" In sudden horror, Lanah realizes that she has forgotten the name of the third girl, who has had the locker next to hers for the last year and a half. Her mind is a blank. Should she:

a. Gasp for breath, clutch her throat, pretend she's dying, and run to the bathroom.

b. Go for something simpler, like faking a faint.

c. Say "This is Michael Jackson, but he's here in disguise so don't tell anyone."

d. Stop the introductions and say, "I have *got* to rescue another guest! Could you each say your name and make Linda feel comfortable?" and then leave the group quickly.

Turn the page for the "Best" answer!

d. Stop the introductions and say, "I have *got* to rescue an-other guest! Could you each say your name and make Linda feel comfortable?" and then leave the group quickly.

Slip into another room of guests, if you can, and stay for a tactful amount of time.

The "Best" Answer:

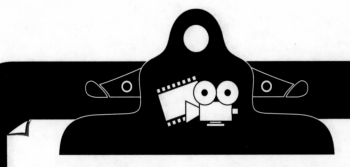

Role-Playing Exercises

1. Stand in front of a full mirror, tall and straight, your feet a little apart, your shoulders back, and your head held high. Pretend the mirror is a new friend, and introduce yourself. Carry on a conversation for five minutes. Try to look relaxed and friendly. Have a friend or family member practice the following introduction exercises with you.

2. Pretend an introduction to a new friend for the first time. Follow the directions to:

- ✔ make eye contact
- ✔ smile
- ✔ shake hands
- ✔ repeat the name

3. Introduce one of your friends to a parent. Look at your mother and say her name first. Example: "Mother, I would like you to meet Tristan. Tristan, this is my mother, Mrs. Henderson."

Role-Playing Exercises

4. Introduce two adults to each other. Have one be a woman and one be a man. Look at the woman and say her name first. Example: "Mrs. Reid, I would like to introduce Mr. Will James. Mr. James, this is Mrs. Schelly Reid."

5. Pretend that one of the adults you are introducing is a very important person. Look at the important person first and say his or her name. Then say a sentence or two about the person being introduced. Example: "Senator Davis, I would like to introduce Ms. Connie Daigle. She is one of the teachers at my school. Ms. Daigle, this is Senator Davis from Claremont, California."

p. 23

Quiz

1. List four places where you use etiquette.

a.

b.

c.

d.

2. Every person you meet, your family, friends, and adults, all act towards you in a certain way because of your _____.

3. Most people are _____, especially young people.

4. List the four simple rules of introductions.

a.

b.

c.

d.

Quiz

5. When you introduce a man to a woman, the _____ name comes first.

6. When you introduce a younger person to an older person, the _____ person's name comes first.

7. When you introduce an important person to either a man or a woman, the _____ _____ name comes first.

CHAPTER 2

Friendship

You've been reading about *meeting* friends. A *real* friend is not someone whom you've just met. A real friend is someone you know well, spend time with, and tell your secrets to. Learn to treasure these friends. The older you get, the harder it seems to be to find the time to make them.

What makes them your friends? They are your friends because they *like* you. They like you because of the way you act towards them — because of your manners.

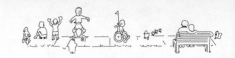

Here are some simple rules to help you keep your friends forever:

1 DON'T WHISPER

Have you ever been in a group of people that started whispering but did not include you? You probably felt very hurt and left out. You may have thought that they were talking about you or that they didn't like you enough to include you. There are always special things you want and need to say to your friends that you don't want others to hear. You should wait until you are alone with them to tell them.

GIVE COMPLIMENTS 2

Let others be happy to be around you. Make them feel special by saying a few kind words. You'll both feel good.

3 DON'T BE BOSSY OR BOASTFUL

Leadership qualities can be wonderful if used in a loving way. Remember when we said that the most important rule of kindness in etiquette is never to correct anyone else's manners? Be kind to your friends and also to others who don't have friends. It doesn't matter if their color or speech is different from yours, or if they go to another church or school. Be kind to them and you'll be a happier person yourself.

4

BE HONEST

Don't lie to protect yourself or pretend you're something that you're not. A good friend will see through it anyway.

BE TACTFUL

5

Imagine you and your best friend are going to a school dance and you have each bought a new dress for the occasion. When you arrive at the dance, your friend comes bounding over excitedly to show you her new dress. Your face falls because it is the ugliest thing you have ever seen! It is bright yellow with a large purple flower on the right shoulder, with green leaves and a stem cascading down the front.

Because she is your friend and you want to be honest, should you tell her how she looks? No. Because she is your friend, you want her to feel good about herself — you might say something like, "*You* look so nice!" If told the truth about the dress, she would probably start crying and hide in the restroom the remainder of the night! Of course *because* she is your friend, you would encourage her never to wear it again. Perhaps you could visit her home before she attends another such event and tactfully find out what she plans to wear. If she is going to make the same mistake, tell her how beautiful another one of her dresses is. Being tactful will help others to feel good around you.

6

KEEP SECRETS

A secret might seem unimportant to the hearer, but to the one whose heart it is held in, it is *very* important. Let's say that Will likes a special girl at school named Schelly. Now Will is quite shy and does not want her to know how he feels. He shares his feelings only with his best friend, Tristan. In his excitement at hearing something that no one else in the world knows, Tristan tells Derrick. Derrick tells his friend Lanah, Lanah tells Laura, and Laura tells...Schelly.

If you were Will, would you ever tell Tristan another secret? No! Tristan didn't mean to hurt Will by telling Derrick, but he did. The pleasure of telling something you know others want to hear only lasts a moment, but the hurt to a friendship lasts much longer.

APOLOGIZE

Learn to apologize when you are wrong or have hurt someone. Then try very hard not to do the same thing ever again. When someone apologizes to you, accept it and be friends again. Should they continue to do the same hurtful thing over and over, you will have to decide if you have made a good choice in a friend.

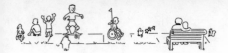

"Let's Pretend . . ."

Tristan Herkelschmertz is just about to go into the new record store at the mall when he hears "Tristan! Hey, Tristan!" He turns to see a grinning boy in a red rugby shirt hurrying over.

Now Tristan remembers that the boy used to be on his soccer team before he moved last year. But he can't for the life of him remember the boy's name. All he can see in his mind is his soccer jersey with the number 12 on the back. Should he:

a. Pretend he doesn't see the boy and duck into the record store behind a Def Leppard display.

b. Say "Wow, you know the team was saying just the other day that it hasn't been the same with old number 12 gone."

c. Say "It's so great to see you again. How have you been?" and carry on as if he remembers.

d. Point to his throat and pretend to have laryngitis.

Turn the page for the "Best" answer!

19

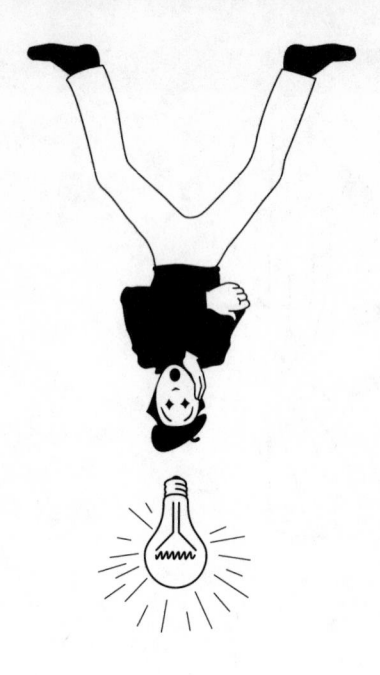

c. Say "It's so great to see you again. How have you been?" and carry on as if he remembers.

   Chances are he will — as soon as the boy leaves.

The "Best" Answer:

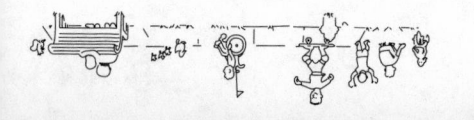

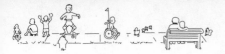

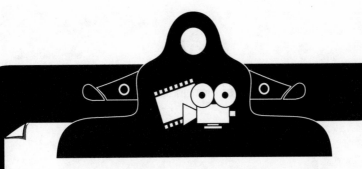

Role-Playing Exercises

1. Compliment friends at school about how they look, or about what they are wearing.

2. Talk to someone in school that you wish you knew better. Introduce the person to your other friends.

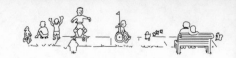

Quiz

1. List the rules of friendship.

a.

b.

c.

d.

e.

f.

g.

2. Why is it rude to whisper in front of other people?

a.

b.

3. Give an example of how you can be tactful.

4. Finish this sentence:

The pleasure of telling something you know others want to hear lasts only for a moment, but the _____

_____

CHAPTER 3

"May I Take a Message?"

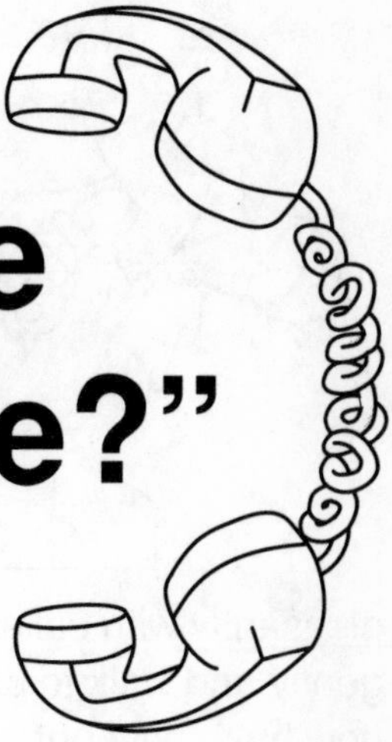

People are very busy, and when they make telephone calls, it is usually for a specific reason. It is very important that the person who is called receives the message.

Answer the telephone in your home by saying "hello" directly into the mouthpiece in a friendly, clear voice. Keep a pad of paper and a pen or pencil by the telephone so you can take good messages. If the person who's requested is not in, write down:

✔ the name of the caller

✔ the phone number

✔ the time of the call

✔ any other message the caller wishes to leave

If you know the person calling, you could take a moment to add a "How are you?" Make sure the messages get to the people called for as soon as they return home. It's a good idea to have a certain place where messages are put in your home.

If the person requested is home, say "Yes, just a moment, please." If you must call out for someone in another room, cover the mouthpiece with your hand. The best method is to chat briefly and pleasantly with callers if you know them, then put the phone down gently and walk to deliver the message. Many phones in the home now have hold buttons. If your phone has such a button, always use it.

Use your most formal manners on the phone at all times, saying "please" and "thank you" often. Use "hello" instead of "hi." Never say "yeah" instead of "yes."

When you make a telephone call and hear a "hello" on the other end, follow the guidelines below:

1. Say "hello," using a friendly, formal voice.

2. State your name. Even if you call often, realize that you are not the only person who calls. Your voice will not be recognized every time, and it is not polite to assume that it will be.

3. Ask for the person with whom you would like to speak.

4. Once your friend is on the line, re-identify yourself.

5. Ask how he or she is.

6. Ask if it is a convenient time to talk.

Because you cannot see your friend, it is very important to follow the last rule, asking if it is a convenient time to talk. Your friend might be in the middle of eating dinner, practicing the piano, studying, or entertaining another friend. The person will appreciate your call much more without feeling guilty about spending time talking to you.

If your friend does turn out to be busy at the time, he or she should offer to call you back later. If not, you might say, "Please give me a call when you're free," or "What would be a good time for me to call again?"

Let's say that you call to invite your friend to a movie that starts in two hours, and you are told that your friend is too busy to talk right now. Say something like, "Please give me a call when you're free, because I want to invite you to see a movie that starts in two hours." This way you tactfully let your friend know that you need an answer very soon, without taking too much time to do so.

CALL WAITING

If you have "call waiting" in your home and during a telephone call the tone tells you that you have another call, say "Just a moment, please," and click over to the next call. Let the new caller know right away that someone else is holding but that you will be glad to return the call when you are finished. Get back to the first call as soon as possible. Never be rude to your callers by cutting them off suddenly to speak to someone more interesting.

If the call was for your brother or sister, be sure to pass along the message when you get off. If a call comes through on call waiting for your parents while you are talking to a friend, be sure to tell your parents before you return to your own call in case they want to take it. If they do, ask the new caller to hold a moment for your parents and tell your own caller that you will need to return the call later.

ANSWERING MACHINES

More and more families are getting answering machines for their home telephones. Something important to remember is that you may leave a message for your friend, but it will probably be the parents who will hear it first. So use your most formal manners and follow these rules:

1. Say "hello."

2. State your name.

3. Say for whom you are calling.

4. Give the day.

5. Give the time.

6. Ask your friend to call you back.

7. Give the phone number where you can be reached, or say that you will be calling back later.

If you do try again, let several hours go by before you leave another message. Then don't leave one unless it's very important.

Do not leave long messages on the answering machine. Some machines only give you 30 seconds to leave a message. Others give you as long as you need up to 30 minutes. Keep your message brief and to the point.

When you listen to the messages on your home phone, remember not to erase them all until other people have gotten their messages, too.

PROPER CALLING HOURS

Carefully observe cautious calling hours by not calling too late in the evening or too early in the morning. During the week, your hours of calling might run from an hour before school starts in the morning to an 8:00 p.m. to 9:00 p.m. cutoff.

On the weekends, never call before 9:00 a.m. unless you have a special outing planned for early that day, or after 9:30 at night. The Sunday evening calling hours return to the weekday schedule.

Let's Pretend . . .

After six weeks of wishing from afar, Morgan Herkelschmertz is thrilled to have Adam Marconi call her. Four minutes into the conversation, another call comes in on the call waiting feature on the Herkelschmertz telephone. The call is from Dartmouth College, which her sister Lanah has been waiting for weeks to hear from about whether her application was accepted. Lanah is upstairs in her room. Should Morgan:

a. Say "She already decided to go to Western State Institute."

b. Realize that her sister's future may be more important than a social call (even from Adam Marconi), ask Adam if she can call him back in a few minutes, and pass the call from Dartmouth on to Lanah.

c. Cut Dartmouth off quickly without saying anything and hope they call back.

d. Say "I'm sorry, she can't talk now. Her parole officer is here."

Turn the page for the "Best" answer!

The "Best" Answer:

b. Realize that her sister's future may be more important than a social call (even from Adam Marconi), ask if she can call him back in a few minutes, and pass the call from Dartmouth on to Lanah.

Role-Playing Exercises

1. Call a friend and chat for awhile, going step-by-step over the telephone instructions. Example:

"Hello?"

"Hello, this is Beau. Is Matthew there, *please*?"

"Yes. Just a moment, *please*."

"Hello?"

"Hello, Matthew. This is Beau. How are you?"

"Hello, Beau. I'm fine, thank you. How are you?"

"I'm fine. Did I catch you at a busy time?"

Role-Playing Exercises

Practice these next two exercises with a family member. Being polite on the phone does not make you unpopular. It makes you an interesting and nice person to talk to. If the friend you are calling does not use the same manners back to you, continue using yours. It will surprise you how fast they will catch on and enjoy the benefits of good manners.

2. Pretend to call friends. Ask if they're busy or if you have called at an inconvenient time, and have them answer that they are busy right now and cannot talk. Respond in several different ways.

3. Pretend that you are calling a friend who is not at home and has left an answering machine on. Leave a message. Ask your parents if you can practice on your own machine at home. It's good to play it back and listen to what you have said. You can really improve your messages this way.

Quiz

1. What two things should you keep by your telephone at home?

   a.

   b.

2. When you answer a telephone call for someone else, what things should you include in your message?

   a.

   b.

   c.

   d.

3. What are three very important words to use when making or receiving telephone calls?

   a. _____

   b. _____ _____

4. List the six steps in making a telephone call.

   a.

   b.

   c.

   d.

   e.

   f.

Quiz

5. State two reasons why it is important to ask if it is a convenient time to talk.

a.

b.

6. Who usually picks up the messages from a family answering machine?

7. What are normal hours to call between on weekdays?

a.m.

p.m.

8. What is the correct time to stop calling on Sunday evenings?

9. What's the earliest you should call on a weekend morning?

CHAPTER 4

Lady and Gentlemen Courtesies

There are certain rules of behavior we follow in social situations to show the kindness and respect we feel towards others. We call these lady and gentleman courtesies. Not only do gentlemen extend these courtesies to ladies, but young ladies and gentlemen extend them to adults, and adults to elderly people. All should learn how to give them naturally and to receive them gracefully. If these seem a little confusing at first, don't worry. Once you start to use these rules, it will soon seem as though you had always known them. In today's society, some of the following rules might be considered for use in formal situations only. You may want to talk to your parents and ask them when they would like you to use certain rules.

1 Gentlemen will open doors for ladies and let them pass through first, and young ladies will open doors for older ladies. The progression through a door might be: a grandmother first, a mother second, and a daughter third. A young gentleman would also open doors for an adult male.

2 Gentlemen stand when ladies enter a room, and all young people stand when adults enter a room. This rule also applies when being introduced to someone and when guests arrive or depart from your home.

3 Gentlemen open car doors for ladies, allow them to enter, then close the door behind them. If a gentleman has let a lady in and they are going to a special dinner or event, she should feel comfortable waiting in the car until he gets out his side and comes around to open her door to let her out again. For everyday manners, the gentleman will unlock and open the car door for the lady, but when they arrive at their destination, the lady will let herself out.

If you ever have the opportunity to ride in a limousine, always stay inside and wait for the driver to come around and open the door. Never open the door for yourself.

4

Gentlemen seat ladies at the table before they seat themselves. They also rise when ladies excuse themselves and when they return to sit down. The gentleman takes care of the lady to his right first. If the lady to his left has no one to seat her, then he will also seat her.

When a lady needs to get up from the table, she should ask to be excused first. The gentleman to her left will get up, come around behind her chair, and let her out. All the other gentlemen at the table will also stand. They will sit back down when she is away from the table. The process will be repeated when she returns.

Do *not* say, "Please excuse me. I need to go to the bathroom." Say something more delicate, such as a simple, "Please excuse me." If looks indicate that a further statement is needed, say, "I need to powder my nose," or simply, "Please excuse me, I'll be back in a moment."

Ladies, help the gentlemen move your chairs by leaning forward and resting your hands on the seat to support the bulk of your weight. Otherwise, it will be almost impossible to move you (no matter how much you weigh!).

Young ladies will not seat their mothers, but will wait until their mothers are seated before sitting down themselves.

5 A gentleman helps a lady with her coat or sweater. Unless the gentleman is holding it, the lady will start putting it on or taking it off first, and the gentleman will see what she is doing and immediately offer and start to help.

Gentlemen, if you have a date, get her coat or sweater and hold it out for her to put on. Put both hands at the top so it is open, and hold it low enough for her to reach her hands into it.

When a lady and gentlemen walk together, the gentleman will walk on the curb side of the street. This courtesy comes from the days when there were dirt roads and ladies wore long, flowing dresses. When the cars rode by, they would splash up dirt and mud so, of course, gentlemen being gentlemen, they walked on the outside. Now they do it for protection. It is also okay for a woman to walk along a window and check her appearance in the reflection. Such behavior is taboo for a man. **6**

When the pair cross the street and change directions, the man will take a quick step behind the lady to get to the outside again. If the man doesn't take the initiative and the lady feels uncomfortable, she should cross in front of him to the inside.

Because this courtesy is one of protection, when young ladies become teens they will need to start doing it for their mothers or any other older women they are with.

7 Gentlemen carry packages for ladies until their hands are full. Only then should a lady have to start carrying things other than her purse. Young ladies should carry in grocery bags for their mothers. Young men who have special friends at school can offer to carry their books on the way to classes, on the way to the bus, or on the walk home.

8 Young ladies and gentlemen stand and give up their seats to adult ladies or elderly gentlemen in crowded buses and waiting rooms. You should never be seated until your mother is seated.

9 A gentleman stands behind a lady going up an escalator and in front of her on the way down. He goes first down the escalator to protect her in case she should lose her balance and tumble down. As you get older and taller, you should do the same for your mother.

10 Ladies enter an elevator before gentlemen, and the older ladies enter before the younger. When the door opens on the next floor, the whole group steps back to make room for others coming in. When a gentleman arrives at his floor, he exits and stands briefly to the side with his arm across the door until any ladies wishing to exit on his floor have done so.

11 If a lady drops something, a gentleman or a younger person will reach down and pick it up for her, saying, "Here, let me get that for you" as he or she walks quickly to help.

Whenever a gentleman has a female guest visit his home, he will always walk the lady to her car when she leaves, whether it is in the day or evening, and open and close the car door for her. **12**

Gentlemen, you might be shy about first trying these courtesies, but you will find that young ladies love it and will start reacting towards you in a better manner. If you ever come across one who does *not* like it, an appropriate reply might be, "I'm not doing it because you are a woman. I'm doing it because *I'm* a gentleman."

In time, these lady and gentlemen courtesies will become second nature. You will do them without even thinking, but they will be greatly appreciated.

Let's Pretend . . .

Lanah Herkelschmertz is dining at Chez Hoity-Toity with her friend Margo Witherspoon, Margo's parents, and Margo's brothers, Dorkmund and Nerdley Jr. She desperately needs to use the restroom but waits until the end of the first course of watercress soup.

"Excuse me, please," Lanah says, gathering up her linen napkin.

None of the gentlemen at the table pay any attention.

Lanah backs her chair up a little on the plush mauve carpet and repeats "Excuse me, please," a little louder this time.

Margo's father and brothers turn and smile at her and don't budge. Should she:

a. Turn beet red and run to the bathroom.

b. Turn to the gentleman to her left and say "Stand up and let me out, please!"

c. Realize there are no gentle-men at her table, smile, and quietly rise to depart for the restroom.

d. Kick the shin of the nearest brother under the table and point to her chair.

Turn the page for the "Best" answer!

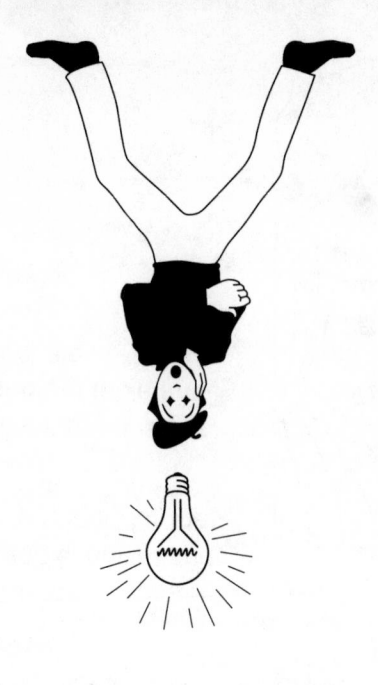

c. Realize there are no gentlemen at her table, smile, and
    quietly rise to depart for the restroom.

    In fact, once she says "Excuse me," she should not hesitate
    at all and should start to pull out her own chair immediately.

The "Best" Answer:

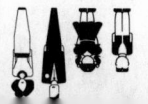

Role-Playing Exercises

Ask several friends or family members to practice these exercises with you.

1. Choose one person to play a grandmother and one to play a mother. With a door in your home, practice opening it and letting the grandmother pass through first, the mother second, and you, as the youngest, third. Rotate who plays whom. Switch the mother to a father, and have him open the door for the grandmother and daughter, or have a son hold it open for his father and grandmother.

2. Have several people sit down in a room and start talking. Play a young lady entering the room. All the men should stand as you enter and are seated. If you don't wish to sit down, thank the men for standing and ask them to be seated. Have a man or woman adult enter the room. All the young people should stand.

Role-Playing Exercises

3. Go to your dining room table and practice these steps:

Boys: Stand directly behind a chair with both hands grasping the chair back. Slide the chair back until the lady can sit down. Once she is seated, push the chair in slightly. Make sure you don't cram it in too tightly. She can always adjust it later. Release the back of the chair and sit down at the table in the seat to her left.

Girls: Stand to the left of the chair you expect to be seated at. Once the chair has been pulled out, sit down, grab the sides of the seat, and lean your body forward while the chair is being pushed in.

4. Pretend that one side of the room is a street with an imaginary curb alongside it. Have a lady and a gentleman walk it, the gentleman on the outside and the lady on the inside. Then have the street side change and the gentleman walk behind the lady to change places.

5. Practice each of the lady and gentleman courtesies with your family members and friends at school.

Quiz

1. What are lady and gentleman courtesies?

2. Not only do _____ extend this behavior to _____ but young _____ and _____ extend them to_____ and adults to _____ people.

3. When a lady and a gentleman ride down an escalator together, who should go first?

4. When a mother, grandmother, and daughter go through a door, who should go first, second, and then third?

1st _____

2nd _____

3rd _____

Quiz

5. At the table, the gentleman will take care of the lady to his _____.

6. Why should a lady lean forward when she is being seated or helped out of her chair?

7. How did the custom of the gentleman walking on the curb side of the street start?

8. What is an appropriate reply to someone criticizing a gentleman for his manners?

Manners at Home

Manners start at home with your parents, brothers, and sisters. You have already heard a lot about manners at home from your parents, such as not spending too much time on the telephone when someone else is waiting for a call, sharing your toys with your brothers and sisters, and compromising on certain television programs that you might want to watch. Of course you've also learned lots of table manners such as chewing with your mouth closed or not putting your elbows on the table.

Let's talk about more manners you can use at home. How about the way you speak to your parents? How do you answer when your mother calls you? Do you say, "Not now, Mom" or "What do you want?!" Your mother and father deserve as much respect as any other adult. One way to figure out if you are talking to them correctly is to compare how you talk to them to how you talk to your teacher. If you talk to your teacher with more respect than your parents, you need to consider changing your behavior at home. Things will go much more smoothly. Remember that people will react towards the kindness you show in a positive way — even your family members!

Another way you can show your parents respect is by using some of the lady and gentleman courtesies at home.

✔ You can offer to carry in the groceries for your mother.

✔ You can open doors for your mother and let her pass through first. Gentlemen, you would also do it for your sisters and father.

✔ You could stand for your parents and any adult guests entering or leaving your home.

✔ Young gentlemen can seat their mother and sisters at the table and stand when they excuse themselves and when they return.

As you get older, you will realize how important your family is to you. Yet it is very easy to take them for granted now. Yes, your parents will always love you, but how about making them *happy* that they love you and *happy* that you are there? When was the last time you told your mother how nice she looked, or thanked her for the meal she just cooked, or for working hard to support you? When was the last time you told your mother that you loved her?

And don't forget your father! Have you ever thanked him for providing all the wonderful things in your home? Have you ever told him how handsome he looks when he is all dressed up? Fathers like to hear compliments just as you do.

Your brothers and sisters are people, too. You may not always get along with them, or even think you enjoy being with them, but you probably won't be getting away from them anytime soon. They're part of your family and deserve the same respect that other people do. You might be surprised to see how much nicer they are when you are pleasant to them. It would probably help to realize that if your best friend lived with you for a year, day in and day out, you would end up fighting as much with each other as you do with your brothers and sisters. Once you have grown up and are out of the house, the times you get to spend with your family will seem very special.

The reason you have problems now with your sister or brother is that you don't have much privacy. You're always together. To help with this, you might try these simple suggestions:

1 If a member of your family has his or her door closed or locked, knock before trying to enter.

Don't assume that your older brothers or sisters want you to join them when they have friends over. Wait until you are invited. If you are the older sister or brother, invite your younger one in sometimes when it does not interfere with what you are doing. **2**

3 Never get into diaries or letters unless you are asked. *Ever.* For no reason should this rule be broken.

4   Don't listen in on telephone conversations.
Would you want someone listening in on yours?

Don't play a cassette or wear a special
shirt of your brother's or sister's that you
don't have permission to just because he
or she is not there.   **5**

6   Don't search through someone else's
drawers without permission.

Relationships between brothers and sisters are never perfect
when you still live at home, but if you practice these principles, it will
go much more smoothly.

Don't all of these sound like things you would like others to do
for you? Perhaps if you start doing them, they will also.

Let's Pretend . . .

Morgan sits across from her brother Beau at the Herkelschmertz dinner table. Beau often chews with his mouth open, giving Morgan an interesting new view of dinner. Morgan is grossed out. Should she:

   a. Say "Eeeeew, gross! Mom, make him stop!"

   b. Think up something even grosser to do back at him, perhaps involving her left nostril and the butter knife.

   c. Explain to him in a sincere tone that although she is *sure* he does not realize it, he tends to chew with his mouth open, which is rather unattractive. Suggest that he practice chewing with his mouth closed, and when he slips up, very gently remind him again.

   d. Ask to be seated beside him instead of across from him.

Turn the page for the "Best" answer!

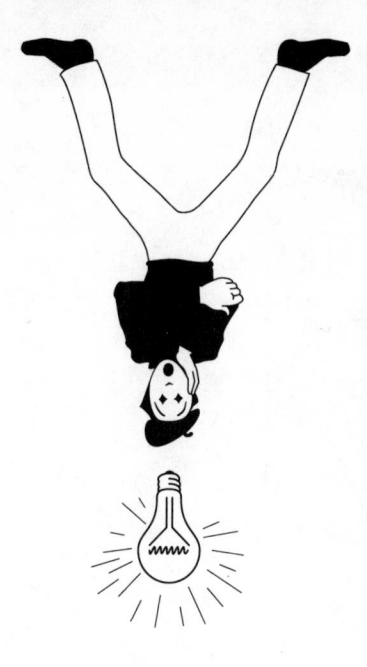

Try "c" first:

c. Explain to him in a sincere tone that although she is *sure* he does not realize it, he tends to chew with his mouth open, which is rather unattractive. Suggest that he practice chewing with his mouth closed, and when he slips up, very gently remind him again.

   The kind, caring approach is definitely worth a shot but brothers don't always listen to sisters. In that case, accept the fact that you've done all a sister can do without starting a major fight, and then try "d":

d. Ask to be seated beside him instead of across from him. That way, at least you won't have to watch!

The "Best" Answer

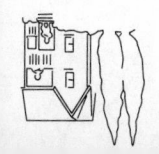

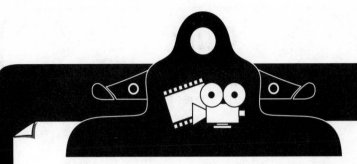

Role-Playing Exercises

1. Compliment each of your family members at least once during the week.

2. Use the following lady and gentleman courtesies listed at home as often as possible:

✔ carry in groceries or any packages

✔ open doors

✔ stand for adults entering or leaving rooms

✔ seat the ladies at the table

3. Follow other lady and gentleman courtesies not listed above that would go well in your home.

4. Practice one whole day of treating your brothers or sisters in a respectful and kind way. The *whole* day. No matter how they act to you.

Quiz

1. What rule can you use to see if you are speaking with the proper tone of voice to your parents?

2. List several ways to respect the privacy of your brothers and sisters.

   a.

   b.

   c.

   d.

3. List some of the lady and gentleman courtesies you can use at home.

   a.

   b.

   c.

   d.

4. Should you wait to be invited before you join in with a friend whom your brother or sister is entertaining in your home?

5. Why is it important to be thankful to your family members?

CHAPTER 6

Friends In Your Home

There is nothing quite so fun as entertaining *your* friend in *your* home. And even though friends don't expect special treatment, it's always nice to plan ahead to make the visit especially nice.

Here are some things you might do:

1 When your friends first arrive, welcome them in warmly. When you open the door, smile at each friend and say something like, "I'm so glad you're here! Please come in! You look wonderful!" They will already feel happy they have come to visit even before they are through the door! If they're good friends of yours, touch them by squeezing their arms or taking both hands in yours. Ladies might even like to give a friendly hug. Watch how your parents greet their guests. Don't be embarrassed about showing excitement that your friend is there. That makes a friend feel good and welcome.

Let your friend be greeted by the first host or hostess of the home, your mother and/or your father. Do not say, "Would you like to come say 'hello' to my parents?" or "My mother wants to talk to you." Your friend might be too shy to go, or might think the parent wants to have a serious talk. Say, "Come in and say 'hello' to my mother. She is anxious to see you," or "She is looking forward to meeting you." Your friend will now feel special. **2**

3 Have a little snack or a special drink prepared to offer your friend. Visitors are usually shy so instead of asking, "Would you like something to eat?" take the initiative and say, "I've made some great cake! Let's have some." Make it sound delicious.

If your friend has never been to visit, give a short tour of
your home. As guests know it is rude to wander around
without permission, they would appreciate knowing
where the restrooms are, as well as the area where you
will be having your visit. It's also a good time to show,
for example, where your parents' room is, although you
would not take a guest into their room without permission. If there are any other areas of the house that are
considered off-limits, this would be the time to handle
telling your friend. Of course you would want to say it
tactfully, perhaps as "We don't usually go in here unless
we're with my parents." Don't say, "We're not allowed in
here, so don't go." After you have shown your friends
around, they should feel at home.

4

Then go and have a great time, but do keep in mind that as a
host/ess, it is your responsibility to keep your friend enter-
tained and happy. Since it is rude for a guest to ask for food
or drinks, keep them on hand and offer them every once in a while,
depending on how long the visit is. Remember, the reverse will be
true for you when you are the guest at a friend's home. Stop and
think about what makes you feel comfortable when you are the
guest. Do each of those things for your guest.

Let's Pretend . . .

Beau has invited a new friend, Erik, over to visit after school. He has his new Nintendo game all set up and ready to go in the family room and can't wait to play it.

Erik rides his bicycle up the Herkelschmertz' driveway and finds Tristan playing basketball. He parks his bike, catches the ball on a rebound, and starts playing basketball with Tristan.

Beau, expecting Erik to arrive any time, checks out the window and sees him playing basketball. Beau smiles and waves. Erik flicks a quick wave and goes up for a layup.

Half an hour later, Beau is still waiting inside with his brand-new Nintendo game while Erik plays basketball with Tristan. Should Beau:

a. Join in the basketball game, and not invite Erik over again unless Beau wants to play basketball.

b. Demand that Erik come inside and play Nintendo with him.

c. Tell Tristan Mom wants him to take out the garbage now.

d. Sneak out and let the air out of Erik's tires.

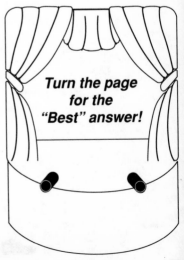

Turn the page for the "Best" answer!

The "Best" Answer

a. Join in the basketball game, and not invite Erik over again unless Beau wants to play basketball.

Role-Playing Exercises

1. Call a friend, and invite him or her over for an afternoon visit.

2. Make something special to eat before your friend arrives.

3. Follow all the steps on how to treat your visitor.

4. Make a list of things that make you feel welcome in a friend's home.

Quiz

1. List the four steps to entertain a friend in your home.

    a.

    b.

    c

    d.

2. In what three ways can you give your friend a warm welcome?

    a.

    b.

    c.

3. Should you offer your guest food or drinks more than once?

Why?

CHAPTER 7

Let's Have a Party!

Parties are fun and a very important part of our lives. Having a party is entertaining, whether it's in your own home, at a special restaurant, or even at school.

I'm sure you have had your own parties. Your parents probably helped you plan them, but once your friends arrived, they were *your* guests and *you* were the host/ess to them.

There are many different kinds of parties, such as those we have to celebrate holidays, birthdays, weddings, anniversaries, school events, and business events. A birthday party is probably the first kind you think of, because it is customary for young people to celebrate the fact that they are a year older. But don't forget the many other holiday parties you can hold. And why not plan a party just to have a party?

THE GUEST LIST

Once you've decided what kind of party you will have and what day you will hold it, a guest list will need to be prepared. A guest list is a list of all those whom you are going to invite to your special event.

Here are some things you will need to consider:

1. How many people you invite might have to be determined by what kind of party it is. If you are having a slumber party, you won't be asking 50 people. You would ask the number that could comfortably sleep in your bedroom, family room, or room of your choice.

2. Decide how many people can fit into the room(s) that you are holding the party in, and do not invite even one more person on the assumption that not everyone will accept. Sometimes they do!

3. If you will be inviting both girls and boys, invite the same number of each. (Obviously, you would not do this for a slumber party!) If you had 10 girls and 2 boys at your party, the boys would end up feeling very shy and insecure. An even number helps everyone relax and feel comfortable.

4. A party is a good time to pay back a social favor. Let's say that a friend invited you over to his or her house. You had a good time but not really good enough to want to return the invitation by entertaining the friend for several hours in your home by yourself. By inviting this friend to your party, you are repaying the invitation.

5. Have you ever wanted to get to know someone better but didn't know how or were too shy? Invite that person to your party! You can get acquainted in a relaxed, casual atmosphere. When you first invite a new person, you might mention some of your mutual friends who will be attending. Then the person will be sure to come.

Guest List

GIRLS

1. _____

2. _____

3. _____

4. _____

5. _____

BOYS

6. _____

7. _____

8. _____

9. _____

10. _____

If you will be inviting both girls and boys, invite the same number of each.

THE INVITATION

There are almost as many different kinds of invitations as there are parties. You can make your invitations, have them formally printed, buy the kind that comes ready-made in packages, or even just call on the telephone and invite your guests.

If you are having a formal party, such as a wedding, you would need to get the invitations out a month in advance. For a more casual party, the invitations need to be received two weeks before. While you are still young, you can get away with sending a birthday invitation a week before, but a longer time is always appreciated. If you decide to have your party at the last minute, by all means call. It's the quickest, easiest way to get people together informally.

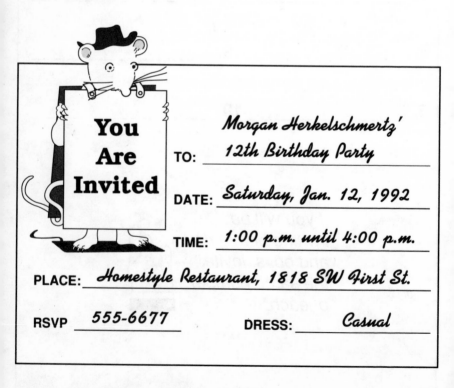

You Are Invited

TO: _Morgan Herkelschmertz' 12th Birthday Party_

DATE: _Saturday, Jan. 12, 1992_

TIME: _1:00 p.m. until 4:00 p.m._

PLACE: _Homestyle Restaurant, 1818 SW First St._

RSVP _555-6677_   DRESS: _Casual_

Your invitation should include these things:

1. **WHAT KIND OF PARTY IT IS**

   Morgan received an invitation to Lara's party. The invitation said to bring a sleeping bag and a bear. She accepted, took the necessary items, but was quite embarrassed to find that everyone else had brought a sleeping bag, a bear, *and* a birthday present. What should the invitation have mentioned? It should have said that it was Lara's *birthday* party, not just a slumber party.

2. **WHAT KIND OF DRESS IS APPROPRIATE**

   I'm sure at one time or another you have arrived at a party dressed in a suit or party dress only to find everyone else in jeans or shorts. At that point, you can either tell everyone you are on your way to another party and will just be dropping by, or you walk in with your head held high and pretend you are a prince or princess and you cannot dress like everyone else. It's best to leave early and not try to play the charade too long.

   Remember, if you are the host/ess, go out of your way to make a guest who has not dressed appropriately feel comfortable. By that time it doesn't matter whose fault it is.

3. **THE DAY, THE DATE, AND THE YEAR**

   Sometimes a person will look at a date and think it falls on a different day of the week. When you list both the day and the date of the party, it makes it very clear.

4. **THE PLACE WHERE IT WILL BE HELD —
   WITH AN ADDRESS**

   If you are holding it in your home, you might want to include a simple map for those who don't know how to get there.

5. THE TIME THE GUESTS SHOULD ARRIVE AND THE TIME THE GUESTS SHOULD DEPART

You will want your guests to know what time to come, and your *parents* will want them to know what time they should go home.

6. RSVP WITH YOUR ADDRESS OR PHONE NUMBER

The abbreviation RSVP stands for a french phrase: répondez s'il vous plâit, or respond, please. The phone number or address beside RSVP lets the guests know they should call or write back right away to the host/ess to say whether they can come or not.

If you are going to have a party with both ladies and gentlemen invited, and a gentleman calls and says that he is unable to come, it would be a nice idea to invite another gentleman in his place to keep the party even. Of course, the reverse would also apply. You will also need to know the final number of guests so you know how much food to provide.

If you are having a large party and do not want to have a large number of phone calls, you can write "Regrets Only" on the invitations. This is normally done when you know most of the guests and assume that they will all come if they can. If you get an invitation that says Regrets Only, you do not have to call unless you will not be attending.

Whether an invitation says "RSVP" or "Regrets Only," it is important to call as soon as you know if you will be attending, in order to give your host/ess as much time as possible to plan the party.

THE MENU

All parties should include food and drinks, even if it is only for a get-together a few hours in the morning or afternoon. If you are having a casual party that does not include a meal, your menu would include hors d'oeuvres such as crackers, chips, or snacks like those that you have when you get home from school. Don't forget lots of drinks, too.

Have you ever heard the statement, "The way to a man's heart is through his stomach?" It's the way to anyone's heart — and comfort. Remember that most people are basically shy, and if they have something to do like hold or eat food, it makes them more comfortable.

MENU

Event: Dinner Party
Drinks: Sparkling Cider
Date: January 17, 1992
Time: 6:30 p.m.
Place: The Table Restaurant
1616 S. Main Street

Courses: 3
   Appetizer Course:
   Chips and Dip
   Main Course:
   Prime Rib
   Dessert Course:
   Black Forest Cake
Condiments: Yes
Rolls/Butter: Yes

Keeping that in mind, let's discuss a more formal party menu. When having a sit-down dinner, you can have as many as seven or eight courses. To keep the menu simple, there are only three required courses for a nice dinner or luncheon menu: the appetizer course, the main course, and the dessert course.

If you are planning a party of eight or more people at a restaurant, you need to call ahead and prepare this menu with the maitre d´ or chef. They get very frustrated when they have such a large group order different foods at once if they are not prepared. An important goal of a restaurant is for all of the people in one party to be served their food at the same time. You can imagine how hard this would be if twelve people each ordered different things that took varied times to prepare.

Also, restaurants do not usually set up tables for service for eight or more without special arrangements. A casual restaurant may good-naturedly try to "make do," but the table you are given and the service you receive will certainly not be as nice as when you plan ahead!

THE SEATING CHART

Once everyone invited has RSVP'd and you have a final number of guests, you should make a seating chart for your luncheon or dinner. Here are some guidelines to follow:

1. As far as possible, it should be lady - gentleman - lady - gentleman.

2. The host and hostess of the party will sit at opposite ends and at the heads of the table. If there is only a host *or* a hostess, the guest of honor would sit opposite the host/ess, the guest of honor being someone celebrating a birthday or visiting from out of town, someone elderly, or an important person. If there is no guest of honor, just seat the most logical person there according to the guidelines.

3. Someone who is a good conversationalist should be seated next to a guest who is quieter so everyone will be encouraged to talk. On your guest list, put Q's next to the quiet guests and T's next to the more talkative ones to help you remember.

4. Best friends, relatives, husbands, and wives should not be seated next to each other — again, so they will have a chance to speak with more people. It's too tempting to only speak with those you know best.

   During the Renaissance period in Europe, they had a very strict etiquette rule that allowed them only to speak to the person on their right during one course and then to switch to the person on the opposite side for the next course. We certainly don't have such a peculiar rule today, but the idea behind it might be a good one to remember. Make sure that if you are a guest, you speak to people on either side of you.

5. A very shy person should be seated next to the host/ess so he or she will feel more comfortable.

6. If you are pairing guests off, remember that the gentleman should take care of the woman to his right, so you will want to put him to the left of the lady you are pairing him with.

7. If you have friends with similar interests, pair them off at a table. Before they sit down, be sure to mention it to them so they can discuss it.

Seating Chart

Hostess

Shy Boy

Quiet Boy

Talkative Girl

Talkative Girl
(Tennis Player)

Quiet Boy

Talkative Boy
(Tennis Player)

New Girl

Quiet Girl

Brother of Hostess

Talkative Boy

Guest of Honor
(Birthday Girl)

Seating Chart

_____

_____   _____

_____   _____

_____   _____

_____   _____

_____

PLACE CARDS

A dinner party with over eight guests needs to have some seating cards prepared. Seating cards or place cards are small pieces of paper that have the name of each guest on them and are put at the place where that person is to be seated. Place cards can be either folded over or set up against a small prop. They can be found at stationery stores, or you can make decorative ones yourself.

Having seating cards will help each guest know where to go, but if you have invited a large number, it is still a good idea for the host/ess to stand near the table with the seating chart, directing them to their seats.

Let's Pretend . . .

Lanah Herkelschmertz is invited to the homecoming dance by Joe from the swim team. She has been wishing for the past week that Matthew, her cute lab partner in physics, would ask her. So far they've mostly talked about equations over the wave tank, but she knows he doesn't have a girlfriend and she's still hoping. Still, she likes Joe okay and would rather go with him than not go at all. Should she:

    a. Ask Joe to wait for two weeks to see if Matthew will ask her.

    b. Say yes to Joe and cancel if Matthew asks her.

    c. Say yes to Joe, and go and have a great time.

    d. Say no to Joe and hope Matthew asks her.

Turn the page for the "Best" answer!

The "Best" Answer

Either c or d would be correct.

c. Say yes to Joe, and go and have a great time.

or

d. Say no to Joe, and hope Matthew asks her.

If Lanah wants to take the risk of missing the homecoming dance in the hope that the boy she really wants to go with will ask her, that's fine. She must realize, however, that taking the risk is her decision and she is responsible for it, not Joe.

Role-Playing Exercises

1. Plan a dinner party for 12 to be held at your favorite restaurant.

   a. The guest list should include several family members and lady and gentleman friends.

   b. The invitation can be bought or made.

   c. Plan at least a 3-course menu.

   d. Make a seating chart.

   e. Make place cards.

2. Plan an informal get-together at your home.

   a. The guest list should include 20 of your friends.

   b. Make the invitations.

   c. Plan a menu that includes hors d'oeuvres, finger sandwiches, and drinks.

   d. Plan your decorations and activities.

Quiz

1. List four different types of parties.

   a.

   b.

   c.

   d.

2. What are the four basic things you need to prepare when you are going to have a dinner party?

   a.

   b.

   c.

   d.

3. Why should you *not* invite 7 boys and 2 girls to your party?

4. If you can only invite 9, how many girls and how many boys would you invite?

   girls _____

   boys _____

Quiz

5. What French phrase do the letters RSVP stand for?

6. What does it mean?

7. If your party is not a dinner party, would you still need a menu?

Why?

8. What kinds of food are included in the appetizer course?

9. List four of the rules to remember when making out a seating chart.

a.

b.

c.

d.

Quiz

10. Why should you place a talker next to a quiet person?

11. What are place cards for?

12. Should you invite more people than you can handle because you know that not everyone will accept?

13. How many weeks before a party should the invitations be sent?

Formal

Informal

14. When should you pre-plan a menu with the chef or maitre d' of a restaurant?

Why?

Hosting Is Fun!

You have planned your party, the guests are arriving, and you are hosting the event, making sure of each guest's comfort. You will:

1. Greet guests at the door with a warm smile and words of welcome. Let them enter feeling that each is the most important guest of all.

2. If they are carrying coats, purses, or packages, either offer to take them to a designated place, or tell them where they should put them.

3. Lead them to the hors d'oeuvres and drinks. Your guests might be too shy to want to bother you. Don't say "May I get you something to eat or drink?" Gently direct or lead them there and give them a plate and cup to fill. We all feel more like socializing when we have something in our hands.

4. After they have received their drinks, lead them to another guest who has already arrived. If they don't know him, make the introduction and mention something about his school, work, or interests, and stay just a minute to make sure the conversation is going okay. If you don't help start conversations between your guests, you may have many shy people standing by themselves, sipping their drinks and basically feeling miserable.

5. Talk to everyone. Don't just stay with your best friend. You've invited everyone there and you are responsible for all of them. Make sure they feel comfortable by being in conversation groups.

6. If you are hosting your party at a restaurant in a private room, have the maitre d' escort your guests in when they arrive, and greet them at the door. Follow the above procedures for hors d'oeuvres and drinks if you have a reception before the dinner. If not, with your seating chart in hand, greet them and show them where they will be seated, making sure to introduce them to the people on either side of them if they don't know them. If you have chosen to seat them together because of some common interest, mention this to them, too.

From time to time, ask if your guests would like more to eat or drink. It's a good idea to have your hors d'oeuvres and drinks set up on different tables around the party area so they are easy to get at.

When the party is over and the guests are leaving, walk each one to the door, remembering to get them their coats and purses. Don't thank them for coming but say, "I'm so glad you came," or "It was fun! Goodbye!" We hope *they* will thank you for such a wonderful party.

Did I say that being a host/ess was hard work? There is a lot of responsibility, but it's fun and rewarding!

Let's Pretend . . .

Tristan has six of his friends over for the night. They've been having a great time watching a game on TV in the basement rec room, playing the stereo, and stuffing themselves on popcorn, sandwiches, taco chips, bean dip, and anything else not moving in the refrigerator.

Around 1:00 a.m., after Saturday Night Live is over, his hockey buddy Anthony decides he wants to go swimming in the backyard pool. All the other guests follow Anthony up the stairs to slip out the back door. Tristan's parents are sleeping, but he knows they would not allow this. Should he:

a. Ask them to be quiet so his parents will not wake up and no one will find out.

b. Talk the boys into playing poker or watching MTV in the house instead.

c. Let the boys go swimming but not join them, and tell his parents later that it wasn't his fault.

d. Tell them his sister's physics experiment contaminated the water and they don't have enough wetsuits to go around.

Turn the page for the "Best" answer!

b. Talk the boys into playing poker or watching MTV in the house instead.

You are responsible for the behavior of your guests in your parents' home.

The "Best" Answer

Role-Playing Exercise

1. Get several family members together and have them role-play with you as guests at your party. One by one, ask them to knock on the door and follow the steps of greeting, entertaining, and making sure your guests stay in conversation groups.

Quiz

1. When your guests first arrive at your door, what should you do to make each one feel like the most important guest of all?

2. Should you be concerned if your guests are not talking to anyone?

What can you do about it?

3. What are the five important rules to entertaining your guests at a party in your home?

a.

b.

c.

d.

e.

4. Why are food and drink important at social functions?

5. Should you thank your friends for coming?

6. What are two things you can say to your departing guests?

a.

b.

CHAPTER 9

Table Basics

By learning and practicing the basic rules of eating properly when you are young, you will automatically use them without even thinking. You'll look better when you eat, neater, more graceful, and more sure of yourself.

Wherever you eat — at a restaurant, someone else's home, or your own home — you should always come to the table with a clean face, clean hands, freshly combed hair, and clean clothes. Not only will you look better to those who eat with you, but it is also much more healthy. A lady may wear her hat at the table if it is a dress hat that goes with her outfit. A gentleman never wears a hat at the table.

Do not sit down before any of the adults. If there are men and women at the table, the man would seat the woman to his right. Once she is seated, if there are any left standing, he can seat them or at least remain standing until all the ladies are seated.

THE NAPKIN

Once you are seated, quietly unfold your napkin and place it in your lap so that there is still one fold in it facing your stomach. The napkin goes directly on your lap. Only if you are eating ribs or lobster are you allowed to tuck it into your shirt collar.

A lady should touch her napkin to her mouth before she takes a drink to remove any lipstick or crumbs that would leave a mark on the glass. Large red lipstick marks on the rim are very unattractive.

If you take a bite of food that is too hot for you, don't make a big scene by fanning your open mouth with both hands. Put your napkin to your mouth and pretend you are wiping it while you quietly breathe in and out to cool your food.

Napkins are also great for hiding mistakes such as bites that are too big. Instead of letting the world see you chew like a chipmunk, pretend again that you are wiping your mouth and keep your napkin there until you have successfully chewed your food and swallowed it.

If you need to be excused from the table, place your napkin neatly on the left side of your plate, or in your chair. Do remember, however, if it is in your chair, to pick it up *before* you sit down.

POSTURE

Your posture at the table is important. Sit up straight with both feet flat on the floor. Ladies, you may cross them at the ankles. Both hands should be in your lap when you are not eating. Don't lean against your chair. When you take a bite of food, don't lean into your plate, but lean across slightly. This way it won't go into your lap if it spills.

Elbows may be on the table only when there are no plates of food in front of you. When you are finished, do not push them out of the way; wait for the waiter to remove them. If he does not notice, you might motion for him to come over. Once the plates are removed, if *necessary*, you may put your elbows back on the table.

SILVERWARE

The easiest rule to remember about what piece of silverware to use first is to always use the one on the outside, and work your way closer to the plate with every course. For instance, if soup is the first course, your soup spoon would have been set on the outside. If you were eating the salad course before the dinner course, your salad fork would be on the outside of your dinner fork.

SERVICE

You will be served food from the left side by your waiter. If food is being passed around, the host/ess will give it to the guest of honor to the right. The food continues to the right around the table until it returns to the host/ess, who serves him/herself last. Your dirty plates will be removed from the right side.

WHEN TO BEGIN

Once you have your food, wait until your hostess has lifted her fork or spoon and started eating before you do the same. If there are more than eight at the table, she may ask you to go ahead. You should do as she asks so your food will not get cold.

One good reason for waiting for the hostess to begin is that some people start all meals in their home with a blessing. This would be said before eating and after you have received your food. Bow your head quietly. If you do not agree with the custom, simply sit quietly out of respect for the host/ess.

THE SOUP COURSE

The soup spoon is larger than the common teaspoon and is held in your right hand with the thumb on top holding it securely. The soup spoon is tipped *away* from you to scoop each bite. Do not slurp or clink the spoon against your teeth! When most of the soup is gone, tip the bowl *away* from you to catch the last spoonful. This soup and bowl action is very practical because if it is going to spill, it will only go on the table, not on your clothes.

Between bites, when you put your spoon down, put it on the plate under the bowl, not in the bowl. This is called the resting position. If you are at home eating a casual meal and there is not a plate under your bowl, you may leave the spoon in the bowl. Otherwise, you must leave it on the plate underneath.

BREAD AND BUTTER

The butter knife will be placed across the top of the bread plate with the sharp side facing down. If you do not have your own butter knife, use the regular dinner knife and rest it on the dinner plate

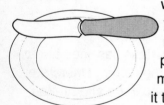

when you are through using it. Never use your dinner knife for butter unless you do not have a butter knife. Take a larger portion than what you need at that moment so you don't have to keep asking for it to be passed.

Put the butter on the bread and butter plate, never directly on the bread. *Tear* off a small piece of bread — never cut your bread with a knife — and butter that one piece, replacing the butter knife across the top of your bread and butter plate. Never do it in mid-air or over your dinner plate. Keep all bread action over your bread and butter plate. Never move your bread and butter plate in front of you. Keep it where it was placed.

HAPPY EATING

With all your food, take *small* bites, chew carefully with your mouth closed, and don't speak until the food is almost gone.

Have you ever taken a bite of food and had someone ask you a question right away? You probably smiled embarrassedly and held up your finger signaling them to wait for just a minute. If you take small bites, especially when you are with a group of people you need to talk to, it's much easier to answer quickly. You can also learn to speak with just a little food in your mouth. Besides looking better, it is also safer to take small bites. Food won't get stuck in your throat as you try to hurry it down.

If you have taken a bite of something you don't like, don't make a face or say "Ugh!" Since you have taken only a small bite, it will be much easier to just swallow quickly.

While you are eating, talk about things that make others happy. It should be a pleasant social experience. The dinner table is never a place to discuss problems you might be having with someone you are eating with (a sure-fire cause of indigestion).

EATING STYLES

When using forks and knives, there are two proper styles of eating: the European (or Continental), and the American. Try both and decide which style you will use. Then stick with it. Practice until it becomes second nature, and don't change. If you are left-handed, you might feel more comfortable eating European style as most of the eating is done with the fork in your left hand.

THE MEAT COURSE: AMERICAN STYLE

When eating meat, hold the dinner fork in the left hand to spear with the tines of the fork facing down. Spear the meat in a small corner. The knife, held in the right hand with your forefinger pointing down the handle, should come behind the speared meat to cut by sawing back and forth. Once the meat is cut, lay the knife down on the plate — not across, but with the top part on the inside and the end out over the edge of the right side of the plate, blade side facing in.

With the tines of the fork still facing down, transfer it to the right hand and turn it so that the tines are facing up. Bring it to your mouth.

If the meat is tender and you don't need to cut it with your knife, use the fork to cut it with your right hand, bringing it to your mouth with the tines facing up. Do not cut more pieces than you need for each bite. This may seem like slow work but it will help you to eat slowly, take small bites, and be able to converse better with those around you.

All other food on your plate can be eaten the same way. Remember to keep the fork in your right hand if you don't have to cut anything.

THE MEAT COURSE: EUROPEAN STYLE

Follow the same directions for the American style until you have cut and speared the piece of meat. Keep the fork in your left hand, with the tines still facing down, and take the bite up to your mouth. Keep holding your knife in your right hand approximately one inch over the plate.

Even though the other food on your plate is probably softer than the meat, you can still use the knife to push the food onto the fork. The tines must remain *down*. With time and practice, you will be able to eat most foods this way. To finish those foods you cannot eat this way, lay your knife down and hold your fork in your right hand with the tines facing up.

THE FISH COURSE: AMERICAN STYLE

Since fish is generally a softer entree than meat, the fork and knife are smaller and the knife is held differently. It is held in your right hand with the index finger resting lightly on the top of the side of the knife, much more delicately than the meat knife. The handle of the knife rests on the *top* of your hand rather than inside, similarly to how you hold a pencil.

Cut the fish with the knife and *push* it onto the fork. Lay your knife down on the plate with the blade side in. Transfer the fork to the right hand and take the bite up to your mouth. If the fish is soft and you don't need a knife, hold the fork in your right hand with the tines up. It is proper to hold the fork in your left hand only when you are using a knife.

THE FISH COURSE: EUROPEAN STYLE

Follow the directions as for American style until you have pushed the fish onto your fork. Then take the bite to your mouth in your left hand, keeping the tines of the fork facing *down* and holding the knife in your right hand approximately one inch over the plate.

THE SALAD COURSE

The salad course can also be eaten with either style, using the meat course directions.

THE DESSERT COURSE

If the dessert is soft, like ice cream or pudding, you should eat it with a spoon. Pie, cake, or fruit is often served with both spoon and fork. If you eat American style, choose whichever one is most comfortable — preferably the fork (tines up) — and hold it in your right hand. The European style uses both utensils. Hold the fork in your right hand. Cut and/or push the bite onto the fork with the spoon held in your left hand.

RESTING/FINISHED POSITIONS

Anytime during the meal that you put your fork or knife down, you will want to place them in the resting position. The end of the fork will be off the left side of the plate with the tines facing up if you are eating American style and with the tines facing down if you are eating European style. The knife crosses under it from the right with the blade towards the inside of the plate.

When you want to signal to the waiter that you are through, put your fork and knife in the finished position. This is a side-by-side position with the tines of the fork down if you're eating European style or up if you're eating American style. Place the knife beside it with the blade facing the fork.

If you drop your fork or knife, do not reach down and pick it up. Motion for a waiter to bring you another, but do it as quietly as possible so that the whole table will not be disturbed.

RESTING/FINISHED POSITIONS

American Style

Resting
Fork across knife, tines *up*.

Finished
Tines *up*, side-by-side.

European Style

Resting
Fork across knife, tines *down*.

Finished
Tines *down*, side-by-side.

FINGER BOWLS

Often before a dessert course, you will be given a plate holding a
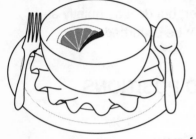 small bowl of warm water with a slice of
lemon in it. This is a finger bowl.
Take it off the plate and place it to
the top left of your place setting.
Sometimes there is a paper doily
under the bowl. This should be
moved also. Use both hands to
pick them both up at once. If there is
a fork and spoon on each side of the
plate, put the fork on the table to the left of the plate, and the spoon
to the right. The dessert should then be served on the plate.

When you have finished your dessert, dip your fingers in the
finger bowl *lightly* (It is *not* a bathtub!) and wipe them on your
napkin or a towel provided for that purpose.

Finger bowl and dessert plate
when properly placed.

TOASTING

Toasting another person is a very special honor. On social occasions, it is generally the duty of the male host unless there are only ladies attending. A toast is given either at the beginning of the meal or at the beginning of the dessert course, when everyone's drinks have been refreshed. The host will raise his glass and say

something appropriate for the evening — a short statement in praise of an honored guest or any others there. If a guest would like to make a toast and the host has not offered one, he would wait until the dessert course and ask him first.

For the first toast, all the guests except the person being toasted raise their glasses, clink the glasses of those nearest them, and take a small sip of their drink. If they have no more drink in their glasses, they would go through the motions as if there were.

For the second toast, the guests need only raise their glasses to the toaster and the person being toasted. It is quite rude to refuse to join in a toast, so be sure your reasons are very good if you choose not to!

After the first toast, it is customary for the guest to return a toast to the host.

Very often at dinner your glass will be the kind with a tall, thin stem. The proper way to hold it is to have your fingers around the stem only, not around the bowl part where your drink goes. This keeps messy fingerprints off the glass, and it helps to keep your drink colder, too.

TABLE DON'TS TO REMEMBER:

- Don't get up from the table until your hostess rises or until you have asked to be excused.

- Don't push your plate away when you are done. If you are uncomfortable with it there, ask for it to be removed.

- Don't laugh if you accidentally burp. Say a simple, "Excuse me, please."

- Don't blow your nose into your napkin. Use a handkerchief. If you don't carry one (and you should!), excuse yourself and use the tissue in the bathroom.

- Don't put your arm on the back of your chair.

- Don't lean back against your chair. Sit up straight.

- Don't leave your spoon in your coffee cup or soup bowl.

- Don't flap your elbows out like a bird when you eat. Keep them close to your sides.

- Don't have both hands on the table when you are eating. Keep one hand in your lap.

- Don't under any circumstances, at any time, *ever* chew gum, at the table or away from the table.

By learning and practicing the basic rules of eating properly when you are young, you will automatically use them without even thinking.

Let's Pretend . . .

Beau is invited to a family dinner at his friend Stefan Burford's house. He is told that Mrs. Burford has prepared a very special meal with all the family favorites. She whisks in the platters and passes them around. First come chicken livers sautéed with onions and garlic. Beau takes a small helping and hopes that the next platter holds something he likes better. Next are pairs of deep-fried frog legs, still joined at the hip. Accompanying them is a bowl of limp mustard greens. Beau simply cannot stomach any of it. Mrs. Burford is watching him anxiously, waiting for a compliment on her cooking. Should he:

a. Push the plate away in disgust and announce that he does not like this food and will not eat it.

b. Throw the food under the table a little at a time and hope that the dog finds it.

c. Take teeny, teeny bites of as much of the food as he can, and cut up the rest and spread it around so it looks like he has eaten some.

d. Announce that he just happens to be allergic to internal organs, amphibians, and green slimy things.

Turn the page for the "Best" answer!

The "Best" Answer

c. Take teeny, teeny bites of as much of the food as he can, and cut up the rest and spread it around so it looks like he has eaten some.

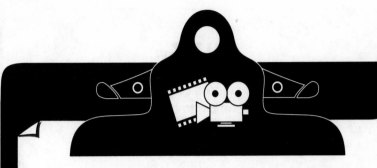

Role-Playing Exercises

1. Ask your family to have at least two family dinners a week.

2. Practice each of the table manners listed.

3. When your family enters the dining room, practice all of the lady and gentleman courtesies before sitting down and when being excused.

Quiz

1. What table manners can you practice before even coming to the table?

2. When you use your eating utensils (forks, spoons, knives), do you go from the inside out, or the outside in?

3. List the different functions of the napkin.

a.

b.

c.

d.

4. Should you scoop your soup spoon towards you or away from you?

Why?

Quiz

5. It is not proper to make _____ ing noises when eating soup.

6. Do you break off your bread or cut it neatly with a knife?

7. Do you butter each piece before you eat it, or butter the whole thing when it is first served to you?

8. It's okay to butter your roll over your dinner plate. (circle one)

True

False

9. Is the fish knife held differently than the meat knife? (circle one)

Yes

No

How?

Quiz

10. What are the two proper styles of eating?

    a.

    b.

11. What is the fingerbowl used for?

12. Name five of the "don'ts."

    a.

    b.

    c.

    d.

    e.

CHAPTER 10

Holiday Gift Giving and Receiving

The custom of giving gifts has been with us since the very beginning of time, and if carried out with thoughtfulness, it remains one of the nicest and warmest acts we can do to let another human being know they are cared for.

"It is the giver that makes the gifts precious," says an old Latin proverb. The thought you give in choosing or making the gift and the manner in which you present it can make even the most inexpensive gift very special. The real value of a gift is not in how much it costs, but in the kind sentiments of the person giving it.

Holiday gift giving is easier and much more efficient if you start it at least several months ahead of time. Early planning also means you can shop around for special sales, which can save you money or allow you to buy nicer gifts.

GIFT LISTS

Keeping good records every year of the people you *received* gifts from and *gave* gifts to is a must. Start your own holiday gift book or file to save this information.

To prepare your gift list, find last year's records of gifts given and received. If you haven't kept a record of them in the past, ask your mother to help you remember them. Write all these names down on a sheet of paper. Then write down any new names you would like to add to the list. Remember not only your friends and family members, but those who have been kind to you throughout the year, such as your teacher, doctor, neighbor, or mailman.

Gift List

Mom	Perfume	$25.00
Dad	Tools	$25.00
Morgan	Sweater	$20.00
Mrs. Jones	Cookies	

Very thoughtfully look over the entire list and remove the names of those you don't wish to or cannot afford to buy presents for this year. Make a clean list. Even if you cannot afford a gift, a kind card with a special word to the person will mean so much.

Beside each name, write down the gift you would like to buy for that person and then what you think that gift will cost. If you don't have one in mind yet, write down the amount of money you would like to spend. Add these all together at the end. If the total does not fit what you have to spend, adjust some of the amounts, remove some names from your list, or think of gifts that you can make. Remember, it's the thought that counts.

THE RIGHT GIFT

Choosing the right gift for those on your list is very important. Sometimes a hasty, non-personal purchase can lead someone to feel that you might be giving the gift because you are expected to. Corporations might buy five or six hundred gifts — all the same — and send them to people they have worked with that year. These are not given to show how much they care for them, but to let them know they appreciate their business and hope to work with them again. Let your gift show that you think your friend or relative is special and that you want to share a little of yourself with them.

Although it is a nice gesture when an adult gives a gift of money to a young person, it must never be given as a holiday gift by young people. The spirit of thoughtfulness and love cannot be expressed in dollar amounts. And once you have given a gift, you should not brag or mention what you paid for it.

Wrap your presents in colorful paper with shiny bows and attach a card or note. Instead of just writing your name, include a warm, personal message, such as: "Chris, here's hoping you have a very special holiday season with your family. Best regards, Jason."

GIFTS RECEIVED

Each gift you receive should be recorded on a piece of paper with the person's name, the gift, and whether a thank-you was written or phoned. You must write a thank-you note unless you were given the gift in person and you were able to thank the giver then. Even then, a thank-you note is still a written remembrance of your appreciation. If you have thanked the giver in person and you choose not to write, follow up with a phone call to say how much you love your present.

Gifts given at parties also need thank-you notes because there is no way to let each giver know in front of everyone how much you will treasure that gift. To save hurt feelings, you should "ooh" and "aah" over them equally and only reveal by note in the next day or two how very much you loved each present.

THANK-YOU NOTES

A thank-you note should be sent no later than one week after you receive a gift. The sooner you write it, the more sincere your appreciation will sound. Waiting only dulls your enthusiasm as you try to remember how excited you *were* when you opened it.

Not only does a thank-you note let the sender know you really liked the gift, it also says the gift arrived. After a week or so of not hearing, the giver might call and ask if you received it. You will feel very embarrassed for not having called or mailed a thank-you sooner. It's important to remember how much thought is given in choosing, purchasing, and packaging a present. The act of giving a gift is not complete until the giver gets to see or hear the joy of the person who receives it!

Don't disappoint someone who only wants to please you. Sit down right away when your feelings are new. When you do, you will find it is much easier to write.

Although today's society has been improved greatly by word processors, computers, and typewriters, a proper thank-you note needs to be an old-fashioned handwritten document. You could use your computer or word processor to compose the note, but then you must copy it in your own handwriting. Engraved or printed cards must *never* be used to send sincere appreciation. You may write (in pen only) on formal or informal paper, personal cards, or stationery. To make it as neat as possible and to save your good paper or stationery, write the first draft of your letter on lined school paper. Read it over carefully to make sure nothing is misunderstood, make all your corrections, and then copy it onto your final paper.

Try to imagine you are sitting beside the person who gave you the gift and talk to him on paper. Say how much and why you like it — even if you don't (remember the acting part of manners!). If the present was money, don't mention the amount but say what you plan to spend it on or save it for. Although you should always send thank-you cards to everyone who gives you a gift, be especially careful to remember the older relatives in your life. A thank-you written from a young relative means a lot to a grandparent or aunt or uncle.

Following are some examples of thank-you notes:

May 10, 1990

Dear Uncle Will,

Thanks a lot for sending the check for my birthday. I have been wanting a new bike I saw at the bike shop. And with your check and the money I've saved, I should have enough to buy it. You should see it — I think it will be really fast.

I hope you will come to visit soon so I can show it to you.

Love,
Tristan

December 7, 1991

Dear Nana,

I was so excited to receive the box from you! I just love the red dress! It will be perfect to wear at our Christmas party next week.

I wish you could come and be with us, but Dad always takes lots of pictures and I'll send you some. Please write soon!

Lots of love,
Morgan

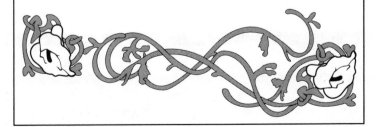

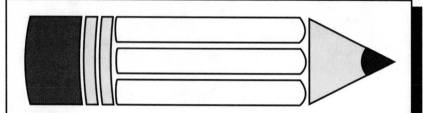

October 9, 1991

Dear David,

Thank you for the great Nerf
football. I love it. My dog,
Sara, chewed up my old one.
I'm so happy to have a new one.
You'll have to come over soon and
play ball.

Your Friend,
Beau

As you can see, these letter samples are not perfectly written documents, but simple and sincere expressions from the heart of how much that gift means to the person who received it.

HOLIDAY GIFTS

When the holiday season is over, all the gifts have been given and received, and all of your thank-you notes written and sent, go back to the lists you made of gifts given and received. There are several ways to store them. You can put them in a manila file folder labeled "Holiday Gifts 199—" and store it in your desk or a family filing cabinet or enter the lists in a home computer. Or you can buy a book from the stationery store with blank pages and label it HOLI-DAY GIFTS. The following pages could be headed with the year at the top, then all the gift information underneath.

These are important records to keep year after year, and not only just to refer to the next season. It is also fun to think of all the memories that were created during that time, and of all the people who have woven in and out of your life.

The real value of a gift is not in how much it costs, but in the kind sentiments of the person giving it.

Let's Pretend . . .

In the glow of the lights on the Herkelschmertz Christmas tree, Lanah exchanges gifts with her best friend Cynthia. Lanah peels the paper from the flat box Cynthia has given her and folds back the tissue inside. She finds a $30.00 gift certificate for Saks Fifth Avenue. Lanah's right brain is delighted; she loves Saks. Her left brain is embarrassed — the gift Cynthia is about to open is a $2.00 friendship bracelet. What can she do?

    a. Not talk to Cynthia for the next month because she is so embarrassed.

    b. Let Cynthia open the gift and then tell her "This is just something to keep until your real present is finished. I'm having it engraved."

    c. Excuse herself from the room quickly and bribe her little brother to come in, grab Cynthia's present, and run.

    d. Thank Cynthia for her thoughtfulness and say over and over to herself "Gifts are from the heart, and she will appreciate it because she is my friend. Gifts are from the heart..."

Turn the page for the "Best" answer!

The "Best" Answer

d. Thank Cynthia for her thoughtfulness and say over and over to herself "Gifts are from the heart, and she will appreciate it because she is my friend. Gifts are from the heart..."

And, if she can afford it, she will realize that this friend is a big spender, and try to do better next time. Perhaps she will get her a special gift for her birthday next month.

Role-Playing Exercises

1. Using the forms on the following pages, do these exercises. You may be able to get the information from past lists. If you don't have any, ask your mother to help you with the names you can't remember.

a. Make a list of people who gave you gifts last year.

b. Make a list of people you gave gifts to last year.

c. On scratch paper, write the names down from Exercises A and B. Scratch off the names of those you don't wish to buy gifts for this year. Add the names of new friends you would like to include.

d. Using the final list of names from Exercise C, make a clean list under the heading "Holiday Gift List 199_"

Gifts Received 199__

NAME	GIFT(S)	THANK-YOU	
		Called	Written
1.			
2.			
3.			
4.			
5.			
6.			
7.			
8.			
9.			
10.			
11.			
12.			
13.			
14.			
15.			
16.			
17.			
18.			
19.			
20.			

Gifts Given 199___

NAME	GIFT(S)	AMOUNT
1.		
2.		
3.		
4.		
5.		
6.		
7.		
8.		
9.		
10.		
11.		
12.		
13.		
14.		
15.		
16.		
17.		
18.		
19.		
20.		

Quiz

1. Is the value of a gift its price?

2. When should you start your holiday gift planning?

3. What are the two gift lists you need to keep every year?

    a.

    b.

4. In addition to your friends and family members, who are some others you might like to include on your list?

    a.

    b.

    c.

    d.

5. Is it acceptable for a young person to give money as a holiday gift?

Quiz

6. a) What is the one circumstance for which you do not have to write a thank-you note?

b) After a personal thank-you, what is the next step?

c) Why is it still important to write a thank-you?

7. If you received a gift at a party and you thanked everyone, do you need to send a follow-up note?

Why?

8. Thank-you notes should be sent no later than _____ after you receive the gift.

Quiz

9. Gifts received in the mail need thank-you notes, not only to let the senders know you liked the gifts but also to let them know that

_____.

10. Should you write a thank-you note in pencil?

11. What are the best ways to save each year's holiday gift list?

a.

b.

c.

Quiz
Answers

CHAPTER 1

"So Nice to Meet You"

1. a) home

b) school

c) restaurants

d) friend's home parties

e) etc.

2. manners

3. shy

4. a) look into their eyes

b) smile

c) shake their hands

d) repeat their names

Chapter 1 (cont.)
5. woman's
6. older
7. important person's

CHAPTER 2

Friendship

1. a) don't whisper
   b) give compliments
   c) don't be bossy or boastful
   d) be honest
   e) be tactful
   f) keep secrets
   g) apologize

2. a) Those not included think you are talking about them.
   b) Those not included think you don't like them enough to let them join in.

3. List an example. Follow the guidelines of rule #5.

4. ...hurt to a friendship lasts much longer.

CHAPTER 3

"May I Take a Message?"

1. a) pad of paper

    b) pen or pencil

2. a) name of caller

    b) phone number

    c) time he or she called

    d) any other message the caller wishes to leave

3. a) please

    b) thank you

4. a) say, "hello"

    b) state your name

    c) ask for the person with whom you would like to speak

    d) re-identify yourself

    e) ask how your friend is

    f) ask if it is a convenient time to talk

Chapter 3 (cont.)

5. a) your friend might be eating a meal with his family, or

    b) he might be entertaining another friend

6. The parent.

7. a.m.) an hour before school starts
   p.m.) 8:00 or 9:00 p.m.

8. 8:00 or 9:00 p.m.

9. 9:00 a.m.

CHAPTER 4

Lady and Gentleman Courtesies

1. Rules of behavior to be used during social situations that show respect and courtesy.

2. gentlemen...ladies....ladies...
   gentlemen...adults...elderly...

Chapter 4 (cont.)

3. The gentleman.

4. 1st) grandmother

   2nd) mother

   3rd) daughter

5. right

6. Otherwise the chair will be too heavy and awkward.

7. The streets were made of dirt and mud and the ladies had long, flowing dresses.

8. "I'm not doing this because you are a woman. I'm doing it because I'm a gentleman."

CHAPTER 5

Manners at Home

1. Compare how you talk to them to how you talk to your teachers at school.

Chapter 5 (cont.)

2. a) knock before entering rooms with doors closed

b) wait to be asked before joining friends your brothers or sisters have invited over

c) never get into diaries or letters unless you are asked

d) don't wear or play with something you don't have permission to

e) don't go through someone else's drawers

3. a) gentlemen seat ladies at the table

b) young people carry groceries for their mothers

c) young people open doors for adults and let them enter first

d) young people stand when adults enter room or house

4. Yes

5. So they won't think you are taking their love and kindness for granted; to make them feel special and happy that you are part of their family.

CHAPTER 6

Friends in Your Home

1. a) welcome your friend in warmly

   b) let your friend be greeted by your parent(s)

   c) offer a snack

   d) give a tour of your home

2. a) smile

   b) say how happy you are to see your friend

   c) physically touch him or her

3. Yes. If friends stay for several hours, they are bound to get hungry or thirsty and it is not proper for them to tell the host.

CHAPTER 7

Let's Have a Party!

1. a) birthday
   b) anniversary
   c) wedding
   d) school
   e) etc.

2. a) guest list
   b) invitation
   c) seating chart
   d) menu

3. The girls would end up feeling very shy and insecure.

4. **girls:** 4 if you are a girl; 5 if you are not

   boys: 4 if you are a boy; 5 if you are not

5. Répondez s'il vous plâit.

6. Respond, please.

7. Yes. Because you will still need to serve drinks and hors d'oeuvres.

Chapter 7 (cont.)

8. Soups, salads, or small portions of entrees.

9. a) lady/gentleman

    b) host or hostess at head of table

    c) talkers next to quiet people

    d) separate friends and relatives

    e) a shy person next to the host or hostess

    f) if couples are seated together, the gentleman would seat the lady to his right

    g) put people with common interests together

10. To help conversation to go evenly around the table.

11. To show where guests are to be seated.

12. No

13. formal: 4 weeks; informal: 2 weeks

14. If you have a group of over 8 people going to a restaurant. Because all the food needs to be served at once and so that you can have a good table.

CHAPTER 8

Hosting is Fun

1. Greet each guest with a warm smile and words of welcome.

2. Yes. Take them over to another group of people and stay until they have started talking together.

3. a) greet them at the door

   b) take their purses and coats

   c) lead them to the drinks and hors d'oeuvres

   d) lead them to another guest to talk

   e) talk with all the guests

4. It makes people feel comfortable.

5. No

6. a) "I'm so glad you came!"

   b) "It was fun!"

CHAPTER 9

Table Basics

1. Wash your hands and face. Comb your hair and put on fresh clothes.

2. outside in

3. a) to wipe your mouth

    b) to cool hot foods

    c) to hide large bites

    d) to get rid of milk or other drink moustaches

4. Away from you. So you don't spill it on your clothes. If it spills, it will go on the table.

5. slurping

6. You break each piece of bread when you are ready to eat it.

7. You butter each piece when you eat it.

8. false

9. Yes. The fish knife handle is held on the top of your hand rather than on the inside.

Chapter 9 (cont.)   10. a) European or Continental
                             b) American

                        11. To clean your fingers.

                        12. a) don't get up from the table before
                               the host/ess or until you have been
                               excused

                             b) don't push your plate away

                             c) don't laugh when you burp

                             d) don't blow your nose into your
                                napkin

                             e) don't put your arm on the back of
                                your chair

                             f) don't lean back against your chair

                             g) don't leave your spoon in your cup
                                or bowl

                             h) don't flap your elbows out when you
                                eat

                             i) don't keep both hands on the table

                             j) don't ever chew gum

CHAPTER 10

Holiday Gift Giving and Receiving

1. No

2. At least several months ahead of time.

3. a) Holiday Gifts Given 199__

   b) Holiday Gifts Received 199__

4. a) teacher

   b) doctor

   c) neighbor

   d) mailman

5. No

6. a) If a gift was given in person

   b) follow up with a phone call

   c) it is a written remembrance

7. Yes. Because there is no public way you can let each giver know how much you really liked each gift.

8. One week.

9. They arrived.

10. No

11. a) in a file

    b) in a book

    c) on a computer

PEP PresS is donating a portion of the proceeds from this book to:

CHILDHELP USA is the largest national nonprofit organization in the United States combating child abuse through treatment, prevention, and research.

CHILDHELP USA HOTLINE
1-800-4-A-CHILD
(1-800-422-4453)

Do You Have Etiquette Questions For Miss Best

Write to her through her publisher and let her help you with your specific etiquette questions. She will be happy to answer your questions personally. Write to:

Dear Miss Best
c/o PEP PresS
114 SW Second Avenue
Portland, Oregon 97204

Watch for Miss Best's column soon to be in your local newspaper.